Once upon a time there lived a y
Adam Black and that young boy is me. I was born in
slough Wexham Park Hospital near maidenhead in
1986 and when I was 4 years old I was diagnosed with
Autism. I lived with my mum and brother when I was
4, my brother was 3 years older then me. When I was
coming upto 1 years old I moved to Dorset my Dad
lived somewhere else when I was living in
Child Okeford as he had found a new partner.
I remember falling a sleep on mums bed before I got
referred to the Maudsley Hospital in London as mum
decided to do a diagnose test because of the fits I got.
As soon as I woke up in the hospital I said what's these
white wires doing on my body, so mum came and
explained them to me. There was a speaker I could
talk into if I needed help on right side of where I was
sleeping. They got a detailed history of my
development and assessed my functioning.
This is where I got the diagnosis from and they were
looking at my Epilepsy to see how that reacts.

During the 1990s I loved watching disney cartoons on my panasonic VHS screen player box that was not for television channels as you had screen on left and could slide VHS tapes in on right hand side of the box. I went to the local primary School and learn't all the basics of everyday speech until I was 4 years old **(See Photo).** *I then started taking tablets that were part of my Epilepsy. When I was little I did plasticine models of colourful heads then I started making models of cartoons I watched and real people.* **(See Photo).** *I liked spinning coins to see if it was heads or tails also loved spinning myself to have a bit of fun in School playground and Swimming pools. I felt happy when I was spinning as it felt like I was being active and had joyful movements come to my emotions.*

When I started local primary school I had no friends as I was still learning the basics of day to day life. I was happy at the school as I liked the routine. In 1998-2000 I got into Playstation one console games like Crash Bandicoot, Crash Bandicoot: 2, Crash Bandicoot: 3 Warped, Crash Team Racing, Crash Bash, Spyro The Dragon 1 2 & 3, Ape Escape and Klonoa as they reminded me of Sonic The Hedgehog that I played on Nintendo when I was young at a friends house. My brother at the same time got into Cool Boarders and Metal Gear Solid games and studied A Level courses at high school. I had a babysitter called Rebecca who looked after me when mum went to pantomine rehearsals for a amateur dramatics company called Snad's who were based in Sturminster Newton. Mum did a number of plays (Lttle Red Riding Hood) (Snow White) and (Wizard Of Oz) **(See Photo)**. me and babysitter played connect 4, Pairs, Jenga, Scrabble and Dominos and had a good time together. When I was 2 years old I was good at Jigsaw puzzles and could turn them over and put them together without looking at the picture.

Mum played Dorothy in Wizard of Oz.

During my early times I was starting to become bothered by the sound of noisy cars and unhappy facials but I didn't know how to express how it made me anxious when was young. Because of that I may have cried a lot when hearing noisy cars and seeing facial expressions that I didn't understand.

When I was 5 years old I went to Yewstock school and stayed there until I was 12 years old. At Yewstock I learned a lot of maths and english and watched historic stories, played musical instruments, History, Geography, Art, Design Technology, P-E, ICT, Diction, Science, Drama and Cooking. I visited my Aunty in Germany who was my mums sister, played pairs with uncle Eric and Jenga with Estrie who is 6 days younger than me. I remember blowing bubbles outside on the balcony, chilled alot and had food there. The first place I got to know my Dad and Lesley was at Lightwater near london as I went there every other weekend. While I was growing up my Dad lived moved a few times to Teddington and Twickenham. I liked to visit my grand parents who lived in Sandbanks.

me and my brother played a bit of football and I sometimes played Drafts and Dominos with Grandpa.I sometimes played crazy golf at Poole Park. My favourite programs were Diggit on GMTV up to Toonattik. I enjoyed all the disney episodes that were showing. I became expert at blowing bubbles, I imagined that the bubbles were cartoon characters. I could blow huge bubbles and manage to blow lot's of little bubbles into the huge bubble without it bursting. I spent alot of time modeling with plasticine which I enjoyed when I saw my family. I also went on holidays with my Brother, Dad and step mother at these places Cyprus, Spain, France, Florida and Corsica which was very adventurous getting to know different beaches and restaurants, I did a bit of parachute gliding and was very brave **(See Photo)**.
When I was 12 I decided to leave Yewstock as it had few bullies that took the mickey out of me and I told people what happened but it carried on and started to feel self concious which led to anxiety.

I went to Beaucroft School when I was 12 which was better as it had an Autism department. I was one of only three boys in the classroom and they wrote the day plans on the white board so we knew what was happening. I stayed at Beaucroft until I was 16 and did go carting of Green Power BP engineer's we called ourselves The Beaucroft Piranha's I also did Food Technology on Wednesdays **(See Photo)**, *Singing in the hall and other lessons was ICT, PSE, Youth Award Scheme, Swimming skills, Careers, Design Technology, Science, English play, Maths, Art, Out in town activities by sometimes leading the way in towns and Athletics. I went on a trip to France and went to the Tank Museum to learn more about the history also went to the Biscuit factory and Cheese factory.*

The school started to build my convidence and I was on a Gluten Free diet having sent a test off to Sunderland University who were researching the effects of Gluten and Casein on people with Autism. It got easier to manage the diet and we noticed that there was an improvement with the Epilepsy.

When I met new people and was in a busy place or table I found it hard to know where to look to handle the new people times, was not sure of how to explain these things to mum at the time as it was in the early stages of not knowing alot of me which is also why I kept things to myself until I could talk to someone who would understand the feelings I get.
My eye contact was also hard as I found it hard to look at new people who might have big eyes.
I had a Social Worker called Richard who was interested to know about my needs and what future I would like, he found a respite carer for me called Jeana who was very nice and kind taking me places and playing card games. I also worked with a carer called Kevin plus a guy called Chris who took me to activities like cinema or bowling. I went to Wing Centre in 2002 - 2005 as Beaucroft had links with them. I found it hard when people called my name out and said okay alright a lot which gave me negative feelings, I preferred the words Good, Cool, Perfect, Excellent and Great.
Mum bought a new black spaniel dog named Beetle (**See Photo**).

I went to the Wing Centre which was a special residential college in the New Forest for young men between the ages of 16-19 with higher funtioning Autism to become more independent. We also had lesson rooms for each subject like numeracy, literacy, relaxation technique's, work experience, citizenship, current affairs, art, wood workshop, cooking, food hygiene, careers, transition, money matters. computers and c.v I was happy there as I had a routine that I liked alot. I also got to know a friend called Bobby Baxter who worked with my Dad and Lesley at Puccino's cafe, he did magician tricks with his finger and he slowly took me to Theme Parks like Thorpe Park, Chessington, Blackpool pleasure beach, Alton Towers and Drayton Maner which I enjoyed as I felt like superman where you went fast and was flying high with a friend close by. I found rollercoasters better as the sound was normal and smooth without the sound of exhaust pipes.

I also got to know friends called Chaylee, Claire, Sami and Kelly who Lesley knew in Maidstone Kent and were interested in me and my console games.

In 2005 I was keen to know the truth about lottery emails you received as I received a number of emails saying about donations and next of kin amounts that I hoped were true and not false. So as time went on I heard that the emails were fake in ways, but I had no evidence to prove if they were true or false so I said to myself instead of wasting luck that could be out there I'm gonna see if they can show me a picture of the amount they will donate and without an expensive postage of over £300 to process funds to know if it's true or false. As I was keen to investigate most things people consider as scams so we are looking more deeper into the evidence truth before we give up.

I got into I'm A Celebrity: Get Me Out Of Here in 2003 which was on ITV1 at Xmas time. Mum started to live with a partner who was called Kevin he also had a labrador dog like we did at the time his was called Gemma and ours was called Fern Kevin was into game keeping places like pheasant shooting and horse racing which I attended to see what it was like. Also when I started to go to Wing Centre college I began remembering my dreams I had like it started off by remembering the good ones then begun to *remember all dreams.*

In 2005 - 2008 I went to Ruskin Mill College which was based near Gloucester a Steiner place with indoor and outdoor workshops like Green woodwork, paper making, felt making, farming, conservation, camping, woodland management, Jewellery, coppicing, leatherwork, cooking, horticulture, Farm shop work experience, computing, weavering, art in nature, speech & language, citizenship and willow workshop **(See Photo)**. *I was living with 2 different House Parents that had a routine plan of what happens each day of the week. Tuesdays was the GYM and wednesdays was either Cinema or Bowling having fish & chips. During my experience I went to the Forest of Dean twice and in my 2nd year went to Sinai Desert in Egypt which was very good camping with Bedoins under the stars in the desert. We travelled on Camels to different camp spots. In my 3rd Year I went to Scotland for The Wilderness Trip* **(See Photo)**. *I also catched the bus during my 2nd year to travel to College and to Stroud town independently.*

Also had a personal tutor on Wednesdays who helped me find an animation tutor to work with.

During September 2007 I started animation drawing sessions with a tutor called Stephen in Stroud I made my first animation film which I finished in July called Football Heroes. Just as I left Ruskin Mill College in 2008 it was a hard time for mum and me as my Step Father Kevin was mostly doing stuff without us and did not understand autism and as mum also noticed he was a bit bossy at points so at the end of 2008 mum decided to split up from him to find a better more arty person. I stayed at mums house until my social worker found an adult placement based in Ringwood St Ives in 2009. So during my stay at mums house I met with a psychologist called Claudia who did an IQ test assessment. My IQ results turned out to be none verbal = 84, which is within the average range and my verbal verbal IQ = 66 of Mild learning disability range, performance IQ = 108 normal range.

I also got to know an Occupational Therapist called Bev who did sensory integration module 2 training with me and I agreed to be her case study to know more about my anxiety and the paranoid feelings I was experiencing. Many of my feelings of anxiety were connected with hearing sudden sounds especially in public places and responding to facial expressions that I could not interpret. Because of this I got butterflies in my tummy particularly when I heard a car with a noisy exhaust pipe drive past the house, as it reminded me of an animal growling back at me rather like the sound of an exhaust pipe talking back. Also during those times I saw some unhappy facials in public which are these **(See Photo)** as when I was very young I imagined public communities to have happy facials and keeping the negative ones private. I began cooking each week at mums house as I knew how to cook for myself independently without needing assistance for getting use to how this or that works. At the start of 2009 it was snowing and I really love snow so I made a snowman in mums front garden next to where the vegetables grew. **(See Photo)**

Facials I find hard and Good ones.

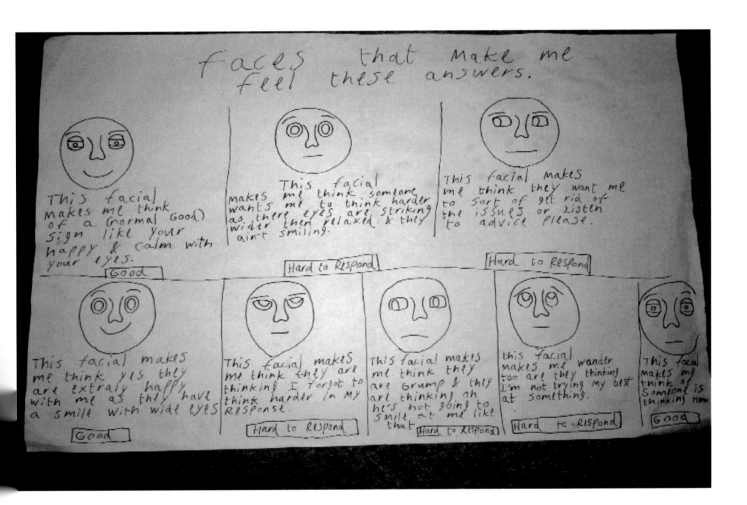

I also made a snow fox. I had been to a special hat shop in Bridport to try to find the right hat for the Raymond Briggs snowman during summer 2009. The lady in the shop very kindly found a green hat and ironed it into shape.

When I moved into my Adult Placement it was not what I thought it was gonna be, as they had strict rules and was not a next door service like if you've got a problem call us next door so they did not seem to understand my autism and sensory needs. They seem to thought I needed a carer all the time when I did not when I was there they took me to visit the St Ives club as I enjoyed playing pool and was good at it.

So during that time I got to know my new social worker called Karen who helped me move back to mums house where I felt safe. I was disappointed it did not workout. With the help of Karen and social services I found a flat that I could live in with support. During my stay at mums house I had different animation tutors help me learn more about 3D modelling.

I went to the Arts University College in Bournemouth to study more on 3D Max Studio software which I completed 3 times I enjoyed going to normal college rather then being with other people with learning difficulties. The tutor there was helpful when I needed support for the software I would put my baseball hat on top of the computer and he would come and help me. I had private tutors who came to the house and helped with Cinema 4D software too after getting to know 3D Max Studio and Cinema 4D I decided to stick with Cinema 4D because all the programming tools had bigger icons to click on and easily remember where each setting was. I worked on a local organic farm as paid work but as time went on I realised that my difficulties were not really understood, for example calling my name out alot made me feel anxious as I preferred quieter voices that were not negative in anyway.

On September 14th during 2009 our labrador dog fern had to be put down as she was not well **(See Photo).**

I also did pottery sessions to learn more about clay and what models I'm looking into making I went to 5 different potters until I found 1 that suited my confidence needs the first potter I went to was good at first but later after a year is was not my kind of place because they prompted me a lot on the things I didn't need prompts for. The second potter I went to was a group of people and sold a penguin for £30 which was the first place I made penguins as I first got into Penguins from a playstation game called Crash Bandicoot and the Penguin was called Penta Penguin. As time went on the potter did not meet my needs because I got told more prompts even though I thought I was capable. I caught the Bus in 2010 with Melissa who was a mental health occupational therapist and went to the gym on fridays to be a bit more healthy and to have more confidence and independence. But after couple of months I no longer wanted to catch the bus as it got very busy and did not suite my needs with a gentleman thinking I took his seat when I had no idea it was his seat and the other passengers were laughing about it. I thought they were laughing at me.

I joined a group through Rethink who support people with mental health issues and got to know Bob who took me and others to play badminton on tuesdays.

I liked Badminton because it is a relatively quiet game, I have been told I am quite good at this as I can make my opponent run around alot and sometimes played pool with Bob who also bought drinks for me at pub I can play pool quite well because I am able to make spacial judgements.

During 2010 I got into gambling alot to see how casino sites worked as I saw bingo sites and fruit machine sites like 888casino as I was not earning money at the time made me get addicted to gambling, the best slot game I loved was Bejewelled as you had to get 3 diamonds in a line which was like Connect 4.

I also tried setting myself limits, so as time went on I heard that gambling was not a good thing as it was only for the rich people compared to lottery tickets.

I had some counselling sessions through Gamcare and learn't that Gambling was not a good thing and expressed my life feelings too.

My social worker tried a number of ways to support me to be independent by sourcing Wessex Autistic Society care package and rowan organisation and learning pathways to find a flat so the final plan was just to put in a bid for an independent flat through the council spectrum signpost.

Also in 2010 it was a cold winter and I was able to make a giant traditional snowman like the Raymond Briggs snowman with a satsuma for the nose and a green scarf and hat during Christmas 2010 as it began to snow at Christmas which was exciting. **(See Photo)** Between 2002-2010 I was visiting my Dad and step mother Lesley in France 3 times a year. Dad lived in 2 different french homes the first one was Bruelle from where they had landed in a hot air balloon while on honeymoon. They moved to the second house in 2004 at Laval which was very peaceful **(See Photo)** After a while I was able to travel independently by traveling from Southampton airport which is smaller and less busy we had arranged the staff to assist me to the plane one day I was wearing my sunglasses to help me manage being in public and the man who came to assist me thought I was blind.

During my France visits I went to different restaurants with Dad and Lesley, And swam in their pool which was fun played on my playstation 2 console by myself and sometimes with my cousin Joshua. Made plasticine models of cartoons I loved and went to Golf centre's where my Dad played with his friends I was an expert finder seeing spare balls in woods and bushes. I got to know a chap called Dave who seemed very nice to me as he bought plasticine for me on one of my birthdays and was interested in me. So as a bit of time went on I heard that Dave took drugs which surprised me even though I got on with him, so we then came to an agreement where I saw him at one off occasions and even saw Mary who was his mum I found out he had been to prison.

Dads work was based around boilers in French homes and Lesley's job was bed and breakfast helping guests feel comfortable. As I love camping I went camping with my dad in 5 different places during those years and they were peaceful sites in france the first camp site was near Rocamadour, **(See Photo).**

I first got into camping when I went camping with mum on Dartmoor when my brother was taking part in the ten tours challenge me mum and fern the labrador slept in a tent.

In 2004 my step mother Lesley had a baby called Lilly who was my half sister and when Lilly was 3 years old she kept saying I love you which I was loving every moment I visited her (**See Photo**). *My Dad got me into Doritos Sweet Chilli that was only available in France and Lesley got me into Caffeine Free Coca Cola so I combined the 2 and it gave a delicious taste I did some research to find out where the best places were to buy them from.*

So as time went on I decided to stay with mum more as mum was getting to know me more within the autism side of things. I joined a Cooking group in Gillingham on every other Wednesdays where I and others took turns on cooking a recipe that we all liked. In Summer 2010 I finished my 2nd Animation film which I showed at mums house using a projector it was called I'm a celebrity get me a log, as I was into I'm a celebrity get me out of here which had funny celebrities who had to do challenging bush tucker trials each year which had Ant & Dec as the presenters. Friends like Laura, Tracy, Jane, Tony and Pam were invited and I cooked my Chilli Con Carne recipe and they all seemed to
enjoy it. I also started to have support workers from Autistic Society who took me places like Tower Park, Yeovil Bowling, Pubs and Cafe's I showed the carers like Michael what Animation clips I made and they liked it (**See Photo**). I went to some events that Autistic Society had going on like pubs from 7pm, bowling, summer barbecue and Xmas disco party in Bournemouth.

At the John Peel Cave Cafe in Shaftesbury Dorset with Michael.

In September 2010 Bev my Occupational Therapist took me to the Great Dorset Steam fair as I was into fast rides that felt like Superman and Bev was keen to see how I managed on rides compared to hearing noisy exhaust cars. we had our own lunch at the fair and looked around **(See Photo).** *As time went on in february 2012 me and mum decided to swap support packages as they were costly from Christchurch to Blandford and importantly I enjoyed working with the carers from Wessex Autistic Society. In October 2010 me, mum, Jude and Laura friends went to Cornwall to stay in yurts at The Park Mawgan Porth* **(See Photo).** *Enjoyed being in the Hot tub with blue light shining enjoyed watching movie with friends which was disney's pixar's UP.*

Also during though's years from 2002-2011 I went to theme parks with Bobby Baxter who my dad knew from puccino's and was a lovely guy. Mum didn't know him at first but soon realised he was genuine and was happy for me to see him. We went to theme parks such as Thorpe Park, Chessington World Of Adventures, Alton Towers, Blackpool pleasure beach and Drayton Manor. The best ones I enjoyed were Thorpe Park and Blackpool as when I went fast on rides it felt like being a superhero like superman also Bob was very funny at times **(See Photo).**

2011 February I went to Centerparc's with mum Jude and Laura friends we stayed in a villa that was cosy and very good (**See Photo**). I enjoyed going on water slides in the swimming pool bit and eating in different restaurants as well. I also loved the tree's as it was set back from the road where I did not hear any noisy cars and the service cars were friendly by letting people cross the road. I went camping in July 2011 at Weymouth Osmington with mum, Jude and Laura, it was very good with the views and sunset in sky. I enjoyed blowing bubbles and having food in a good environment, I had my own pop up tent, lovely sunset (**See Photo**) Jude had her own big tent which they put up. Dad decided to move back to England to Tregony near Truro in Cornwall where he then worked for english boilers and Lesley still did bed and breakfast for guests. When I was living at mums in 2011-2012 I had to spend some time on my own while mum was at work and some of the activities I tried didn't work out I became more anxious and started to use white noise sounds to block the outside traffic sounds along with my soft silicone ear plugs.

I also was changing where I wanted to sleep at the time as my upstairs bedroom was part of the front bit of the house where it got noisy at points. So I said to mum if it was fine for me to make a corner sensory room floor bed close to kitchen and we agreed it could happen as a strategy to see how things went as it was also part of the back of the house away from sounds. The main idea of having a sensory room corner came from when I went to Beaucroft and Wing Centre where Beaucroft had a Sensory Room that me and others used at times and at Wing Centre I did relaxation techniques to help my conscious times, stress ball too. So the next few days I said to mum that I felt comfy and was still dreaming too with the pillows under 2 sleeping bags supporting my back (**See Photo**). *During these times I was seeing a psychiatrist, explaining how and why I wanted to use strategies to cope with day to day life times the psychiatrist and mum was keen to see if drugs like quetiapine would help me cope more without strategies.*

My Sensory Floorbed corner.

As time went on trying different drug tablets I kept getting side effects like being tired alot and getting tears in my eyes often. So I then thought of coming off meds when the side effects occurred which I did a few times, but as time past my mum thought I slightly became un-well using strategies alot, but I knew my strategies were helping me cope alot even though I was using more then I started with.

My strategies were 1. Sleeping on floor in a comfy way from not hearing cars alot, 2. wearing ear plugs to reduce the slightest sounds heard, 3. using an electric wind fan as white noise, 4. wearing disguise glasses was to never have to put up with

*negative facials in public, (**See Photo**) and 5. typing my paranoid thoughts on laptop to feel like I'm secure with my true feelings and to process everything.*

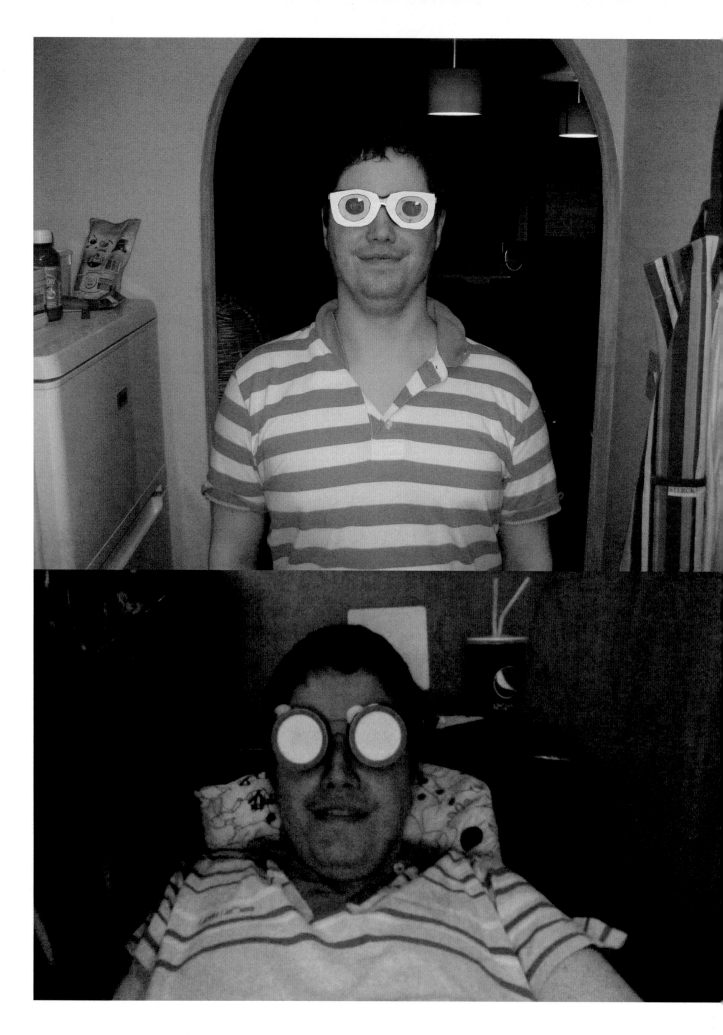

I also catched a Nordcat bus to Grandad's house in Bridport during the rota times where Nordcat did a £10 1 off journey to longer distance places. Me and Grandad spoke about good history times like old photos of him and where he use to go and the photo of me when I was little, his favourite place to go was Westbay near Bridport my mum sometimes says Grandad had some autistic ways. I remember going to different cafe's with Grandad one was near Westbay where it was a train cafe and another one was at Lyme Regis beach where he use to work for preparing the deck chairs for people.

Near the end of 2011 mum decided to listen to me more as she saw similar patients at clouds house and took tablets to help her not feel stressed often which helped me build more trust in mum as I could express myself more which helped her to understand me better. In January 2012 mum had a slight miss understand that she believed my Macbook Pro Laptop would blow up when overheated but I knew it wouldn't as it was the latest technology and the air vents were not covered so we asked a computer guy in Shaftesbury and he said it should be fine as long as the air vents were not covered so mum nicely realised I was correct. In 2012 I was still seeing Melissa care coordinator and playing Badminton with Bob from Re-think.

*In february I started will a new support package called UKSLS which stands for UK Supported Living Services **(See Photo)**. I got to know my first senior carer who was (Phil) he seemed very nice and interested to know more about me like my Animation I was doing so we went to different pubs together for 3 hours. I went to UKSLS office to discuss my support times and activities plus my needs*
David Service Manager seemed very friendly.

In April 2012 I saw an email from a girl called Anita from refugee camp based in Africa who was interested to be my girl friend and ask me to be power of attorney for her so I manage her money. But I heard from Autistic Society that it was a scam but in my mind I was keen to investigate further as Anita never asked for my details or any transactions, also my Autistic brain never wants to give up something until you find evidence to give up so nothing is ever a waste of luck and never a guess job without evidence. So me and David from UKSLS decided to investigate further as a team so we looked into the internet at the UKSLS office and found that the same messages was part of a different name user and the same person, in the end we decided to give up as David and me saw that she was like a scam pastor and obviously she lived in another country.

The activities I started to do with Phil and Tom was finding a Gym on mondays that had no TV screens to help with paranoia side, as I did get paranoid with the facials on TV screens during my experience at other Gyms. On thursdays I got dropped off at Hope 2 Bake from 10:00am then from 2:00pm. This was a cooking activity as I loved cooking new recipes to try out. I went Bowling at Tower Park, Fridays was Hope 2 Bake again as the Cooking Group decided to use there kitchen as the Gillingham bungalow was going to be used for something else, then from 1:00pm was being dropped off at mums.

Saturdays was meeting at Beggars Banquet Cafe with friends of mums with my carer too based in Shaftesbury and sundays going to Tower Park to see a cinema movie from 2-10pm. When I was at Hope 2 Bake I made different cakes like my first one was a snowman type of ginger bread chocolate cake, **(See Photo)** *so as we came upto September 2012 I decided to no longer go to Hope 2 Bake because the kitchen was a small room with too much talking involved and one of the volunteers misunderstood my sensory difficulties to loud sounds like the saucepan dropping by mistake. I then got to know Tony carer who took me to Cinema on sundays and supported thursdays too. In May 2012 I then had my first flat that my Social Worker found through Spectrum Signpost there were two options, the first one was in Gillingham and the 2nd one was in Okeford Fitzpaine. I decided to go with the Okeford Fitzpaine flat as it was quieter then the Gillingham one, so I went to Ikea in Southampton with mum to do some shopping for my new flat. We found a red sofa I loved and a fusion table, a clock and some stripy curtains that I loved.*

This is a Toy Story Birthday Cake Icing I made for a young boy called Alife.

So me and carers were working on doing up my flat by slowly painting the place and getting a blue carpet and cooker along with a washing machine **(See Photo)**, at that time I got to know a new carer called Michael who seemed lovely and smiley.

Once I did up my flat I had my own money pots for each day of the week getting £70 a week of benefits so I had to budget alot as of having less money each week. When I settled in my flat I had same carers who did sleepovers from 6-10pm and finished in morning from 8-10am and sometimes 8-12pm David sent me the staff rota's of each week via email from friday. During the summer in 2012 I was enjoying my activities like Bowling, Cinema, Cooking, Pub and Beach but as time went on Service Manager David said to reduce my activities because of not having the funds to do extra mileage as Rachael from County Hall made a slight change to the weekly costs of only having about £50 of mileage a week. I was cooking Chilli Con Carne at my flat during monday nights which had over 20 ingredients and was one of my favourite recipes.

So when the mileage change occurred I autistically said to myself in order for me to feel like I still have my activities I will need to find a pub that has no problem with me being there 5 times a week until mileage is sorted for other activities. So I went to the Anvil Inn pub and they seemed happy at first saying I can be there all day but as time went on one of the managers said I couldn't bring my own food there as in a cake I made at hope 2 bake which I never knew was going to be a problem as I thought it was to make yourself at home. Also in my early times mum got 2 different pub places to cook gluten free sausages that mum bought along with her. So I was agreeing to not bring my own food there but then I heard that I wasn't welcomed to stay there for the day any longer.

So I asked the Hambro Arms pub in July 2012 if they were fine with me being there when closed but in the front room and for 8 hours and they said yes we have no problem with you being here and you can use the front room when closed from 3-6pm.

I made myself comfortable in the pool table room where a table was and in the front room when closed which was very kind of them. I was offering to buy my first drink and the bar gentlemen called Dan said no you don't need to pay it's free of charge for you. As I heard Dan say it was free of charge I was like Oh my gosh how really generous of them to offer me free drinks. By August I heard from my Occupational Therapist that 8 hours was alot to spend at a pub for the day, so I explained to Occupational Therapist that I was doing it because of not having the funds to do activities yet and that the pub staff have no problem with it after me and carer checked. Also I was refusing to see my Psychiatrists in Feb 2012 as they were always arguing that me using strategies was a sign of Mental Illness which I describe as Paranoid Heath as I was mainly paranoid with sounds and negative facials that got me thinking alot.

I loved using the name Paranoid Health because it sounded more straight forward and less negative as Mental Health as when I was very young I heard few people say this or that guy is Judge Mental plus saying for example this guy is very Mental I don't like him, all of which I heard when I was young at my 3rd school.

So in relation to the Psychiatrists they also wanted me to take Risperidone tablets to see if anything helps but I was more keen on using my strategies that were helping my tummy moments so I felt safer just talking to my Care Coordinator which was Melissa at the time as there were no issues when communicating to Melissa. I was taking Mebeverine to help my butterflies anxiety stomach tummy which was helping and I told Melissa about it and she seemed fine, only the Psychiatrists did not know as I refused to see them as of too much arguing each time.

Also during July 2012 I went camping with Michael from saturday - monday morning by end of July **(See Photo)** as we saved up some mileage just for that activity we camped in Weymouth Osmington was only £10 a night which I paid for.

During my first day there it wasn't very sunny as it rained alot and we just chilled at campsite and had a shower plus made our own foods with a camp cooker. During this time mum found a new partner who was more creative and calm who loved gardening too and that was Gary. at August 2nd 2012 I went to see the Fireworks in Sandbanks beach on a thursday with mum, Pam and Michael carer as when I arrived at the church property car park in Poole with Michael I saw Pam there who I gave a hug to then mum arrived we had a Barbecue and loved the feeling of the sea and all colours of the Fireworks Michael and Pam had chats in the beach hut while I went on my laptop for a bit. Pam was a friend of mums who I've known since very young and she was very kind and generous at times as I played with Play-doh when I was very little at her house and begun to do more plasticine models too during that point.

*Michael
carer*

I also went walking with my Occupational Therapist and Michael around Okeford Hill and we funnily saw a sheep follow us upto the footpath and it wasn't scared of us which surprised us so I took my sunglasses off and stroke it only the others were slightly scared except for 1 sheep.

As the end of October approached the pub manager said this is not your home which I knew it wasn't the only things I was doing at the time was asking if I could have a note saying I am doing Animation here which the bar staff agreed to plus Mark who was a bar staff said I can have a pillow case over my head and people can just ask me if they want so it was agreed as a coping strategy for me which I knew was a bit odd even though it helped me process the busy room times as one offs. The reason I was using a pillow case over head was because when too many people are in a small room it disturbs my concentration like having too much visions to think about when my eye can see more than just a few things moving plus hearing too much too.

I was turning the TV off because I thought no one is watching the TV as no one was in the room watching anything which made me think I can turn it off but the manager said in not a nice way, no just leave the TV on even if we are not in the room.

So as the manager was misunderstanding me alot I decided to leave the pub as of him thinking I was trying to make the place my home when I wasn't, the reason I wanted to go to the pub in the first place was because of not having the mileage money to do other activities and to not feel lonely at flat without going out for the day for a bit of company and as usual having soft drinks and never having any alcohol.

Just as I was gonna leave he barred me and said never to come back which got me confused as the other colleague told him I was already leaving from what I said to the colleague.

So I went to the Langton Arms pub and coincidently bumped into the manager I fell out with and just made myself comfy in the back room where skittles was. 1 day later I unexpectedly saw Bev my Occupational Therapist who said I have an assessment meeting with the Psychiatrist at my flat which I was not aware of. I knew I had a tutor that day but I did not have his mobile to let him know I had to cancel my Animation session so I just had to unexpectedly leave to have my assessment meeting. I wrote some notes for the Psychiatrists as of them misunderstanding as to why they thought I was un-well when I believed I was not un-well by taking Mebeverine that helped my butterflies in my stomach and using strategies to cope in the autism world.

So I unexpectedly got detained in hospital at Stuart Lodge in section 2 of the Mental Health Act and had to take my meds they gave me to try out.

So I wrote more notes as I knew there was alot of misunderstandings going on in relation to my autistic ideas of strategies that the Psychiatrist believed as Mental Illness so as time went on I spoke to a Mental Health advocate and solicitor to help with my issues I had and they seemed very helpful. Bev, Claudia, Mum and Care Coordinator had a meeting with Psychiatrist explaining that my strategies are important to me and that I was trying Risperidone. During my stay at hospital it felt like being in prison feeling like I've done something wrong as I had no idea in the first place that Psychiatrists had the power to detain me in hospital if I thought I wasn't un-well when they did think I was un-well as I thought at the time that I had more choice and control about how and when I wanted to try tablets like the relationship with my GP doctor.

I spoke to my solicitor at the time to arrange my first tribunal which was going to take place at Stuart Lodge hospital. After my tribunal it was decided for me to go on a CTO of Community Treatment Order by having a depot injection this was all decided because the Psychiatrists thought I was not being capable of taking risperidone by myself when at the time I knew my strategies were helping instead and the mebeverine tablets. In 2013 I was still seeing my solicitor to arrange a 2nd tribunal because there was definitely a misunderstanding happening at the time in 2012 like some thought I was withdrawing my activities as it was the money mileage that wasn't in place to do them and I was using my autistic idea plans to go to pub for time being. So by January 2013 my Social Worker Simon got direct payments to fund the mileage costs. I was also seeing my advocate Robin who was telling me more about Psychiatrists and how things work, like he suggested Bose Cancelling Noise Headphones to reduce background sounds so I slowly bought some with the County Hall money and they helped alot.

I then found office space in Blandford Sunrise Business Park as a guy called Steve Marney visited me and others at the Job Club at Stur Quest in Sturminster Newton and told us he did office space. So when I went to Swann Office spaces by Feb I had my Animation sessions there with Moray **(See Photo)** and others along with appointments from Social Services who met me at the Swann Office on wednesdays. By February it began to snow in Dorset so I made a Snowman in the play area field of Okeford Fitzpaine. **(See Photo)** I began watching Broadchurch on ITV mondays as it was a detective program starring David Tennant and based in Dorset West Bay whoch was familiar to me. I went to Freshwater holiday park to use a hot tub on fridays I liked this because of the warmth and the bubbles coming up. I then started to go to the White Horse Pub in Stourpaine on saturdays and wednesdays as the staff had no problem when we asked of me being there for the hours on saturday. I enjoyed having Chicken Madras Curry or Side order of chips on saturdays at pub and watching a movie on Laptop.

I also enjoyed going to Tower Park watching a Cinema film on tuesdays for £4.50 and playing bowling on thursdays at Tower Park. I also went to the Gym on mondays and did Tesco shopping and cooked a mince recipe in evening. I also loved going to the Beach on fridays with my pop up tent as that felt like an activity which Simon Social Worker had no problems with but only David from UKSLS had an issue because he thought I would get detained in hospital by going to the beach again with pop up tent even though me and Simon saw it as an Activity to get out more, The only reason I did it before the hospital was to gain more confidence and go out more and having a romantic feeling like a holiday, some believed I was isolating myself but I wasn't otherwiseit would of happened nearly everyday which it wasn't, just needed a bit of confidence and new peaceful 1 off activity until the mileage is sorted. The reason I pitched a pop up tent in the cold weather sometimes was because when I was at Ruskin Mill College they camped out when it was raining and wanted to see a challenge of the students surviving in rain with bin bags in there rucksack where the clothes could keep dry.

I also enjoyed seeing mum every other Sundays as Gary mums new friend was new in the family and gave a bit of new feel to the process of visiting as we played pairs using cards on table and watched movies we all liked.

So my 2nd Tribunal was in March and my carer Stephen, Solicitor, Mum, Catherine, Claudia, Social Worker and Psychiatrist came to the meeting.

In the meeting I was keen to use my strategies still and possibly go on tablets myself without the depot injection by the end of the meeting it was agreed I can be responsible with tablets and no longer being on a depot. So I would of expected my strategies to still be my main coping method but it turns out I had to wait longer as I started with a new female Psychiatrist who was more smiley and gave me a rough date as to when she was happy for me to come off meds and give my strategies a try again, until April 2014.

During April - September I saw a nurse who use to be a carer with me her name was Clare and she knew about dieting strategies to keep myself healthy. So all in all I was enjoying my weekly routine as it was what I was expecting to happen in 2012.

I was seeing a Ceramics potter who was nice from the start as he had lot's of clay ideas like myself but as time went on I was finding it hard to work with him as I got told the same advice that I was already aware of and he had a difficulty by not remembering what he already suggested to me so I spoke to Patrick my art tutor and explained I wanted to find someone else.

By July Beetle one of our spaniels had to be put down as she was old and poorly and could only walk slow, so I spent some time with mum then I went to visit one of my college friends Philip who lived in Reading and me and County Hall were happy to pay for the extra mileage during my visit, me and Philip watched Monsters University at the Showcase Cinema and I paid for taxi's there and back, me and Philip enjoyed the film. I went camping with Stephen carer at the end of July to Manor Farm campsite which was in Charmouth and it was very good as they had a bar and a food order room where I got Gluten Free Chips and I went to Charmouth Beach on the first activity day at Campsite and went into the sea.

By August 2013 I had a theft issue with my money as I was keen to see my money piles grow in my bedroom so I could still see my money instead of it be in my bank all the time.

The theft began around August 19th - 30th, so I reported money going missing for the first time by telling my carer senior and others like my Social Worker Simon during that stressful time I rang the police and reported it and I got to know a new Occupational Therapist called Tracey who also did a bit of safe guarding, so I told her that the money went missing and who I thought may of stolen it like one of my carers called Jade carer who took my spare house keys and got Kevin carer to return them.

Tracey suggested a meeting with police officer in Sturminster Newton so they were aware of the story and how it went missing from start to finish to do an investigation with carers.

All the carers had discussions with the police officer and said they didn't take the money when one of them must of as it happened not just once but twice when they took a bit of money at the time like I remember thinking I have a £20 missing on 19th August and thought I was miss counting but as time went on by 30th it reduced more from what Stephen and me noticed so I was not miss counting.

As time went on the police officer said the investigation could not continue as the carers knew I had money going missing and they did not know who did it, I was happy to show my bank statement as I did not use the missing money for anything as I showed Tracey my statement at Swann offices the amount that went missing was £360. So I was going to look into a Safe box for Xmas so if I ever chose to save in piles again I would put them in Safe Box with a key to lock it and screwed onto wall.

In September 2013 me and Stephen carer went camping again but in a different place which was Dartmoor just to get my stressful thought's of money going missing a break, so it was very nice and quiet place as we were the only ones camping there **(see photo)**. Went to a local pub in a good village close to campsite and enjoyed different pubs seeing what menu's they did and having a drive around which County Hall appointee was happy to pay for out of my benefits by sending invoices. I also went to the Highway man inn bar near Devon which was like a pub but an old time attractive ancient place that only did sandwiches and pasties plus drinks.

I also started to watch Atlantis on BBC 1 which was the makers of Merlin which I was watching in September 2012 on my laptop at pub and Atlantis was very interesting to watch. In the start of October I went to the London College of Occupation Therapists to do my first Conference talk of my autism sensory needs which went very well in front of alot of people and even sold my pottery models of penguins.

Then stayed at Bobby Baxter's house in Epsom for 1 night and had an Indian Curry, In the past I cooked Rapid Ragu recipe which Bob and Chrissy loved, **(see photo)** *then we watched Shrek Forever After on Virgin TV. In November I got invited to another Autism Conference at Birmingham N-E-C in front of 250 people and felt brave to read my speech out which I enjoyed and sold a few more of my pottery penguins* **(see photo).**

During the end of 2013 I decided to swap banks from Lloyds to Nationwide as there was un-expected overdraft charges when I still was in the right balance place with all my money. So I moved over to Nationwide as they were way better not charging huge fee's and had a dispute system where you could dispute un-expected payments or anyone not giving refunds with evidence pictures. I was slowly going to let County Hall know so they were aware of my bank changing. In October monday 29th 2013 I sadly heard my Grandad passed away as he was good to be with and interested in my news of Animations and talking about what he use to do in the early times.

Rapid Ragu recipe.

So it was a sad time me, mum, Gary, Brother, Aunty and Cousin's came to the funeral and thought of all the good things about Grandad, like I knew he was very generous giving xmas and birthday money each time. During Xmas time we had a very good Xmas as I watched a few movies that we all didn't mind like Doctor Who, The Snowman and Disney's Dumbo.

In 2014 After getting a new bank card and that I heard from my Psychologist Claudia that I had to ask first before changing banks which I forgot was a Power Of Attorney Rule so I had a finance meeting with them and discussed why I moved banks plus Stephen carer attended by supporting me.
I was still doing my favourite activities with my carers each week and during this time I was interested in removing one of my carers who spoke alot about any subjects we chatted about as I only liked the carers who spoke little about subjects and were understanding my needs.

In February I got invited to a Dragon's Den Panel which was a pretend one with lot's of professionals and Occupational Therapists the panel took place in Broadstone near Poole Dorset. So I was 1 of the judges on stage seeing how all the different service people were doing by explaining there ideas and me plus 3 others were voting from 1-10 to see what we thought of their service ideas. So the best one I voted for was Sensory Integration as I was interested to have a Sensory Integration near me and in the end the Audience also voted for Sensory Integration which became the winner of the Dragon's Den Panel.

I also started to have a new Animation tutor called Timothy who knew about polygons, vertices and edges of 3D Modelling, we worked for 3 hours on wednesdays to begin with at Office then as Timothy had a masters degree course on Wednesdays we then decided to have the sessions at the White Horse pub on Saturdays which I guessed was fine as they were having no problems with me being there with my laptop from feb 2013 - feb 2014.

Psychologist also helped me make a Communication Snapshot which helped whoever I was working with to understand and meet my needs. I was using a Kinect Sensor with Moray which senses motions of me moving and 3D object moving at same time as me.

In the summer of 2014 I tried out my Motion Detector that my brother got me for Xmas which came from China and was able to film motions of us walking in and out front door. I decided to do Badminton instead of Gym as the Badminton was more fun than the Gym and we played Badminton at Blandford Leisure Centre for 1 hour then had shower. I went to Studland beach on fridays during the summer when it was sunny with my inflatable blue sofa which attracted people by walking past as they said I like your blue sofa. On the rainy days I decided to go to Tower Park Bowlplex bar on Fridays as Freshwater holiday park had no free wi-fi and became busy in there bar. I went to the Purbeck centre in Wareham to do my conference talk on my sensory needs which was good as few people asked questions and sold few of my pottery models of 1 penguin for £10 and a Jackdaw for £10 and A Snowman for £15.

I also started to work with Karen Social Worker in June who I use to have from 2009-2012 as she came back from maternity leave and I was keen to still work with her so we met up and discussed my plans like changing my support hours. In July I began to come off meds to see what it was like without meds for anxiety and trying mebeverine to see if that supported butterflies of active brain which it did help as I told and explained to my Care Coordinator Liz that I was still happy to do all my activities and that I knew there was more to me in 2012 of the hospital admission. I went camping again with Stephen carer at Moonfleet near Weymouth we set up my Gazebo and pop up tent and went into the camp pub nearby and they offered to do gluten free bolognese sauce with rice which was kind of them.

*On the first day after camping 1 night we decided to go to Charmouth Beach and sunbathe with my inflatable blue sofa (**See Photo**) then we went back to campsite and had sausage rolls for supper all cooked in our secure Gazebo.*

Next day we decided to go to Chesil beach which seemed very peaceful and quiet compared to Charmouth **(See Photo)** *then we went back to campsite and had baked beans for supper during the last night. On 15th August 2014 my mum moved to her new house which was in Milton Abbas and it was a very peacefully cottage which I loved for a change was not as noisy as Child Okeford During the end of the summer I saw an action drama program that I was interested in which was Gotham City on channel 5 mondays and I liked it alot as it was a detective story about batman when he was young.*

In September 2014 I got introduced to a Mental Health Nurse through UKSLS called Jay who seemed very nice and willing to help me.

I did a conference at Yeovil Fiveways Centre with Ros and Bev my Occupational Therapist which was good then by 19th September me and carer travelled to Birmingham Aston University to do a Conference in the Sensory Integration room at Aston University, so we stayed for 1 night in a hotel of the University which was paid through Sensory Integration only Ros could attend but Bev had to go to London to see Kate Bush sing. When I did my talking in the Sensory Integration room there were others doing talks about sensory needs and guys filming the speeches which they filmed mine and I enjoyed it as I made over £100 by selling my pottery **(See Photo)**.*

In October I visited my Dad in Cornwall for the weekend and went out to an indian restaurant did a pumpkin for Halloween and was wearing a fancy dress wig on 31st October.

I was in a relationship with a friend called Sarah who Philip Pearce referred me to in 2011. Sarah was based in Weston Super Mare and was very keen to meet me in Yeovil so we met face to face for the first time in Yeovil as Yeovil was closer for us so we played bowling which I paid for 2nd game and Sarah paid for 1st game. I bought a drink for Sarah and bought one for myself then we went into Pizza Hut which did Gluten Free menu's and had a lovely chat together then me and Stephen carer dropped her off at Yeovil Junction train station and took few photo's.

In December as Christmas approached I ordered presents via amazon and thought of all the things my family would love like I generously bought a Tom Tom Sat Nav for my mum to help with journey's to places. I got introduced to a Social Worker Reviewer lady called Georgia who seemed nice and good so we got to know each other by explaining what I do and what support I'll need in future.

I had a meeting with my Psychologist to discuss relationships and what the law is on being with a partner and what you can do and can't do.

So as Christmas Eve came my bro took me to mums house in a rented van and told me a new meaning that described my needs and that was Metaphor where I find it hard when a word was meaning more then 1 thing like someone saying Okay or Alright is hard to know whether it's someone asking to check I'm fine or just saying it in there own normal accent.

We all stayed in and watched TV and chatted about news and things also had dinner together.

On Xmas day we slowly opened all our presents and mum said she loved her Tom Tom, Gary said he loved his Steam Train wallet, My brother said he loved his Tottenham Hotspurs gifts and my dad liked his present.

I watched a bit of wallace and gromit short films and I loved the gifts my brother gave which was a Red T-Shirt saying I AM AUTISTIC GET OVER IT! a snowman outfit and a Usb Fan that had colours going around like a sensory room **(See Photo)**.

Then on boxing day I went to Tower Park to chill at bowlplex bar with Bhola carer and took all my presents to the flat. During new years eve I went to the White Horse pub with an agency carer who seemed nice and had drinks and celebrated news years day and spoke to Sarah on facebook and said she loved her present I gave her of moving light circles.

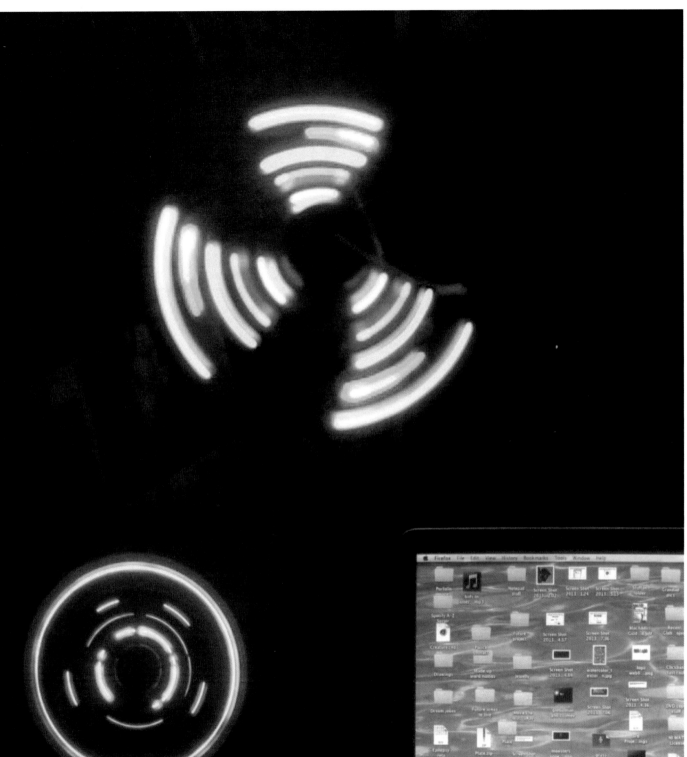

In January 2015 I was still getting to know Georgia Social Worker Reviewer who was helping me with my support hours and removing a carer.

So me Georgia and others had meetings at Mildown Unit every 3 weeks to discuss all agreement plans. Also I did a full IQ test in January with a different psychologist called Liz I scored low for verbal comprehension. I did better than only 4% of other people my age, I scored above average for visual. My perceptual reasoning score was really high and did better than 68 out of a 100 people my age. I scored below average for holding onto information working memory I scored low for processing speed.

By middle of January I successfully removed the carer I no longer wanted and stuck to the ones I liked alot like Stephen and Oliver carer who were very good. At the end of January I began to hear voices in my head during the daytime, so by middle of February I decided to go back on meds to see if it would make a change and it slowly did make a change of not hearing the voices.

I met up with Sarah on valentines day at Poole train station and went to Poole Tower Park to play bowling and had drinks then we went to Chiquito restaurant and had dinner there and chatted for a bit as we enjoyed ourselves.

During February - April I was keen to learn more about Binary Options trading platforms to see if any would benefit me in earning money so I tried a number of different brokers and platforms that are to do with the stock market but as May approached I decided trading was too complicated and was not my sort of business goal. The only online business investigation I'm doing is PTC sites which stands for Pay To Click sites where you click an advert or read email link then wait for the seconds to run out and then you've been credited a certain amount, so time will tell if any of those sites will be successful in paying me.

As my Birthday came up I saw Sarah 2 days before my birthday at Tower Park and played Bowling then went into Nandos and saw Joe who I knew from my last boarding college of Ruskin Mill had a lovely chat and enjoyed ourselves.

On my birthday the activity I did with 2 of my friends plus mum and Gary was go to play Bowling in yeovil then have an indian curry in Sherborne which I enjoy doing and sometimes it's

Skittles and a Curry. In the start of April I was meeting a new care package lady called Nikki from I Direct who met me at the Swann Office and she seemed very nice and smiley and was doing an advert to get new carers for me as we spoke about all the things I currently do and what I would want from the new carers **(See Photo)**.

The reason I wanted a new care package was because UKSLS were getting short staff to cover shifts and was not as good as when I started with them.

On 10th April I went upto Cardiff to meet Sarah for her birthday and chill at her hotel so I went to a bed and breakfast house for 2 nights with Michelle carer who drove me there we did get lost at first but we phoned them up and they gave directions.
So on 11th April I met Sarah at the Doctor Who Experience in Cardiff and we took photo's and enjoyed our visit to the Doctor Who Experience **(See Photo)** *then had a meal in the premier inn hotel where Sarah was staying and I gave Sarah a present of a dogs tale as a hook for hanging coats on plus Sarah kindly gave me a DVD.*

As time went on Sarah decided to leave me to someone else only because of distance living far away to see me regulary so I felt sad she was leaving as I enjoyed her company as we had many things in common like Epilepsy, Autism and Doctor Who.

So during April - May I was still having my regular meetings with Georgia, Liz, Nikki and Patrick at Mildown Unit discussing my support plans and things to think about plus met my 2 new carers through I Direct who I interviewed with Nikki.

Very much looking forward to starting with I Direct soon who will takeover from UKSLS.

My final bit is about my Communication Snapshots I mentioned that I did with my Psychologist Claudia also if you would like to see my Animations on youtube just search my username adamblacky09.

Adam Black

My communication snap-shots

(or everything you need to know about how I experience Autism)

I have difficulties at times with the way people use some words. This has to do with Autism and the communication impairment associated to the condition.

For example, when people say good-bye, I mind if they say "be good" or "take it easy" because I interpret it as meaning that I may not be looking after myself well enough.

I like it when people talk to me about positives and things that are going well.

Using a lot of negatives or 'giving advice' is hard for me as I think it is a criticism of how I am getting on with things. Please avoid using 'no' more than one time.

I like these words: "good", "cool", "perfect", "great", please try to use them instead of 'okay' or 'all right'.

COOL

My difficulties with some words possibly come from the time I was at School and College and they were used when difficulties happened and it stayed in my mind as meaning that something is not right.

I also have problems reading facial expressions. I call this 'facials'. Sometimes people need to explain to me how they feel as the facials alone are hard for me to work out.

Problems reading facial expressions and emotions is again a well acknowledged difficulty in all individuals in the Autistic Spectrum Disorder.

Finally I have very significant sensory processing problems. Again, part of the Autism condition. I am very sensitive to noise (particularly traffic noise), I also find light (sunlight, strong lights overwhelming) so I use some 'strategies' to cope with the sensory issues.

- I wear a hat

- I wear glasses

- I also wear ear-phones that block noise or put some background music to block the traffic noise.

Made in the USA
Columbia, SC
29 January 2022